MIND CONTROL

Manipulation Deception and Persuasion Exposed

2nd edition
Jeffery Dawson

© Copyright 2014 - All rights reserved.

In no way is it legal to reproduce, duplicate, or transmit any part of this document in either electronic means or in printed format. Recording of this publication is strictly prohibited and any storage of this document is not allowed unless with written permission from the publisher. All rights reserved.

The information provided herein is stated to be truthful and consistent, in that any liability, in terms of inattention or otherwise, by any usage or abuse of any policies, processes, or directions contained within is the solitary and utter responsibility of the recipient reader. Under no circumstances will any legal responsibility or blame be held against the publisher for any reparation, damages, or monetary loss due to the information herein, either directly or indirectly.

Respective authors own all copyrights not held by the publisher.

Legal Notice:
This book is copyright protected. This is only for personal use. You cannot amend, distribute, sell, use, quote or paraphrase any part or the content within this book without the consent of the author or copyright owner. Legal action will be pursued if this is breached.

Disclaimer Notice:
Please note the information contained within this document is for educational and entertainment purposes only. Every attempt has been made to provide accurate, up to date and reliable complete information. No warranties of any kind are expressed or implied. Readers acknowledge that the author is not engaging in the rendering of legal, financial or professional advice.

By reading this document, the reader agrees that under no circumstances are we responsible for any losses, direct or indirect, which are incurred as a result of the use of information contained within this document, including, but not limited to, —errors, omissions, or inaccuracies.

Table of Contents

Introduction
Chapter 1: The Concept of Mind Control
   Brainwashing
   Mind Control
   Extent of Effectiveness
   Who Uses Mind Control?
Chapter 2: The Mind Control Process
   Reading People
   Unfreezing
   The Process
   Freezing
Chapter 3: Mind Control Techniques
   Education
   Propaganda and Advertising
   Religion, Politics, and Sports
   Food, Water and Air
Chapter 4: Controlling People with Your Mind
   Know the Personality of the Person
   Four Basic Personality Colors
   The Power of Emotions
      Fear
      Guilt
      Ego

- Addiction
- Anger

Chapter 5: How to be Deceptive?
- How to Conceal?
- Do not Lie; Tell Half-Truths
- The Deception Tool-Box
- Develop a dynamic personality
- Appeal to Everyone
- Humor

Chapter 6: Influence– How to Become a Master at it?
- What are the benefits of influence?
- How to Have your Say in Group Conversations

Chapter 7: Tool-Kit for Persuasion
- Seem Confident
- Do your Research
- Appeal to Emotions
- Use Rhetoric
- Keep Sarcasm to the Minimum
- Sound Reasonable
- Watch Reactions
- Subtlety is the Key
- Cross out the Alternatives
- Suggest!
- Listening
- Observation

Chapter 8: Tips to Play Mind Games
Prefer Half-Truths over Whole Truths
Appear Introvert
Talk less
Hit when the Iron is Hot
Be Selective; Not Choosy
Gain Trust
Chapter 9: What is Manipulation and what are its Benefits?
Moral fix
Chapter 10: How to Manipulate?
Observe
Let the other party speak
The Less you Reveal; the more they Wonder
The best Manipulators are the Best Speakers
Be Subtle
Appeal to Emotions
Be Suggestive and not instructive
Cleverly bring out the negatives
Conclusion

Introduction

Welcome and congratulations! You have chosen the perfect guide to live life on your terms. Here, you will be made familiar with the necessary ingredients to cook up a life full of opportunities to have your way in matters that are important to you.

Not every lie that is spoken is bad. Not every deception that is presented is made with ill intent. Not every mind game that is played is evil. We have come across Disney villains and mega super minds manipulating their way through movies and stories.

We adore them, detest them and yet want to be them. You cannot ignore the character of Severus Snape or Jim Moriarty who were such characters you cannot simply hate just because they possessed something an average man doesn't- the power to manipulate and lie.

In today's world of deceit and lies, it has become relevant to catch up and learn a few tricks of the trade. A man cannot survive solely on the basis of honesty and hard work. While such characteristics are necessarily required, you also need to know where to have your say and more importantly, how to have it.

If life were easy with just the positives and no negatives, it would have been a boring world to live in. The game becomes interesting when you add some spice to it.

Let us then embark upon the journey of how to live a life that is boosted by the power of manipulation, deceit, mind games and half-truths. You are in for quite a journey, indeed!

Chapter 1: The Concept of Mind Control

Most people may initially believe that mind control, otherwise known as brainwashing, thought reform, or thought control, has been around for the longest time. Surprisingly, it had been popularized only recently. It was during the Korean War when the term brainwashing was coined. The word was used to explain why 21 among the 20,000 American prisoners of war (POW) defected to their communist enemies. There was also an incident where some POW's were told to confess something that they did not do -- wage biological warfare.

There is, however, a distinction between mind control and brainwashing. The crowd often interchanges these two very different concepts, but how they work contrasts each other, as you will see demonstrated below.

Brainwashing

Basically, what makes one different from the other is the process undergone by the person being manipulated. In brainwashing, the person is aware the manipulators (or agents) are enemies, and that he is being pushed under the control of these people. In order to survive from the possible physical force being inflicted on him, submission to the imposed belief system is apparent. Should the brainwashing method be discontinued, the victim will soon recover and get his original individuality back.

Mind Control

The process of mind control, on the other hand, is more subtle and the effect is more damaging. In this method, the manipulator enters the person's life as a friend or teacher - an individual worth trusting and believing in. Just from this simple introduction, the victim may have already let all defenses down and may even willingly participate in the mind control process. There may be no physical force involved in this instance, and the victim is under the impression that he is making all decisions by himself.

Mind control aims to change a person to the very core by altering their decisions, perception, beliefs, values, behaviors and relationships. The process is subtle and slow. Oftentimes, the victim is unaware how extensive the manipulation is, if not completely oblivious to it at all. It will, however, involve social and psychological pressure and force.

Because the victims are under the impression that the decision to adopt new values and beliefs is made by them, and the fact that the agent is viewed as a trusted friend, even when the manipulation is discontinued, the new identity will continue to persist. In essence, when people think the changes they embraced are independent resolutions, they are more likely to stand by and even fight for it. This is what makes mind control more dangerous if used for the wrong motives and bad intentions. Its effects are more powerful and it lasts longer.

It is also important to note that though mind control is somewhat unethical, it can be used for good reasons. Some people with addiction issues can be subjected to this process to cure them of their habit. However, you should also be aware that people can use this system on you and that those who are vulnerable to it may just believe that they are following their own instincts, whereby they are following the instincts of the controller.

Extent of Effectiveness

Of course, there's still a chance to undo mind control. However, this will heavily depend on how extensive the manipulation is, or how deep the relationship of the victim and agent is. Some of the other factors that can affect mind control are enumerated in the following:

The number of techniques applied on the victim

- Duration of exposure to manipulation, how long per session and how often
- How deep the relationship of the victim is with his family and friends, and how much interaction and support he gets from them
- Whether the victim is allowed to have outside exposure and how long
- If sexual abuse and hypnosis is utilized
- How much direct contact the victim has with the agent

All of these may sound dark and horrid, but it is important note that all of these can happen in the most innocent-looking setting, like seminars, camps, and other similar activities. Even meeting a new friend and getting too intimately close may lead to mind control. Relationships are often based on mind control to some extent. You may believe that all your interests are indeed yours, though you may find out at a future date, when the relationship is no longer a valid one that they were in fact the ideas of the partner that was strongest mentally and who used control to change the way that a person thinks and the actions that they take.

Who Uses Mind Control?

Cults are the ones that utilize mind control the most, and this is not limited to groups wearing white coats and masks or those who shave their heads to distinct themselves. Even the smartest looking person in a sleek suit can have the intention of manipulation, and even the simplest looking lady with a regular day job can be a member of a cult. These groups have become so sophisticated that all of them will look all too normal. Below are some forms of groups and professions that apply the process of mind control:

- Religions
- Politics

- Philosophy
- Science
- Sports
- Meditation
- Healing therapies
- Personal Development
- Money Making (E.g. network marketing, and stock exchange)
- Psychology

And the list goes on up to, surprisingly, such things as hairdressing.

Basically, everyone can be a victim of a cult, and thus mind control without realizing it. The best thing anyone can hope for is that there is no motive for the manipulator to take advantage of the victim.

It is important to note as well that groups, organizations, and professionals are not the only ones that use mind control. Random individuals can apply these on anyone, and, oftentimes, with the least good intention. Some serial killers and psychopaths use this to hook victims.

How do you know if you are being controlled? The process being undertaken by manipulators will be discussed in the next chapter. However, here is a little food for thought. Do go to a social place of gathering and look around you. How many people do you see wearing jeans? How many people do you see with the same hairstyles? Society itself is capable of using mind control and often does without people really realizing it.

Chapter 2: The Mind Control Process

In most cases, the primary goal of manipulators is to create a clone of themselves -- to have the members of the cult think like them. To achieve this, one must have a high sense of entitlement and a well-fed ego. Having no doubt in oneself is the key to being able to convince people that he is above authority and should be copied. In other words, they will enforce a new personality on their victims.

Everyone can fall prey in this, and it is only a matter of how extensive the mind control was being imposed that will determines its success, or how deep it will change a person.

Basically, almost all manipulators follow a series of steps to successfully impose their will on individuals. This has been proven over and over by the many networking marketing companies actively recruiting people to sell their products. All new members undergo a systematic training on how to recruit people and how to make target buyers make a purchase, and it compares oddly close with the mind control process.

A basic outline of the mind control process is provided and explained below.

Reading People

Of course, before anything else, the agent must first establish a connection or bond with their victim. As explained before, with friendship as the foundation of a relationship, all psychological and social defenses of the victims will be put down.

Manipulators opt to understand their targets before making efforts to bond. This will allow them to know the person's possible weaknesses, interests, and strengths, and use it to strike sensitive nerves -- an essential process to move on to the next step of mind controlling.

How do they do this? Generally, agents will assess a person through first impressions, and this assessment is accurately supplied by body language. People keep three personas:

(1) Private Persona,
(2) Public Persona, and
(3) Reputation.

The first one contains an individual's inner personality. It is the character that lives inside his head, and is composed of thoughts, attitude, preferences, hopes, ambition, values and emotions. The second one is the person people project. Here, positive traits are conspicuously displayed, while negative ones are toned down. The third one is how people perceive a person, thus he has no control over it. Basically, this is the foundation of the first impression, and it often lasts a long time, if not forever.

Agents will read through this and assess your value and usability. If they find you apt for their needs, or if they think you will prove to be a good follower, they will then proceed on knowing your strengths, weaknesses, insecurities, needs, values, and anything they can use as leverage. Afterwards, based from their assessment, they will transform themselves to a person they think will appeal most to you to get your attention and your trust. All of the agent's actions will convey these four basic messages:

➢ I like your personality
➢ We are the same
➢ You can trust me
➢ We are good for each other

Of course, there are times when all of the abovementioned steps may not follow each other in strict sequence. Some may overlap, while others may overtake. Whatever it may be, it basically depends on the situation. Nonetheless, these comprise the first step of the mind control process -- establishing a connection.

Unfreezing

Everyone has a semi-fixed set of values and beliefs that they garnered since childhood, and have lived by up to adulthood. These have become a part of a person's identity, and when questioned or contradicted, the natural reaction of the individual would be to stand by and defend it.

When these established values and beliefs are questioned by the person himself, he is undergoing what's called unfreezing. Many situations can trigger this; the loss of a beloved, getting fired from a job, remittance of a house, and any other incident that can make a person seek reassurance, question his beliefs, distrust people, and doubt the system.

Once an individual undergoes this period of emotional vulnerability, he becomes the perfect target of manipulators. As explained in the preceding step, they will use a person's weakness to their advantage, and they will say everything he would want to hear.

A typical example of this is when a strong minded man gets together with a woman who has very little self-confidence and insists in imposing his will on her on the pretext that he loves her, cherishes her and wants to protect her. Often, in relationships such as this he will know all the right things to say in order to give him power over the situation and to feel in control.

The Process

The main objective of this stage is to unweave the person from his past because this will allow him to let go of his established values and beliefs, and acquire those from his manipulators. Apart from distance, however, the agents will also make the preceding events of the victim's life bad, wrong, or the cause of their hardships. This way, the person will have no way of defending himself or his understanding of the world before, making him susceptible in accepting new concepts and ideas.

As for the methods used in mind control, it is necessary to have the victim isolated from the outside world during the process. This means that agents will make full use of seminars, focused group discussions, or even one-on-one meet-ups within the manipulators' territory. If they can, it is ideal to place their target/s in their environment twenty-four hours a day to have strict control over the person's activities. There are some who will intentionally weaken the victims' body by limiting and restricting their food intake.

Some methods require the victims to participate in the mind control process late at night. The brain is tired during these hours, causing the person to bypass critical thinking and simply agree with whatever is being said or educated by the manipulators. This may be coupled with public confessions -- probably the most powerful tactic to unfreeze victims. The person will lose his sense of privacy, merge with the group unhealthily, and this will make him more vulnerable to other methods of mind control.

Keep in mind that all private information can and will be used to break the person further down. Humiliation and insult will be expressed subtly by the leaders of the group or by the manipulators to leave the victim/s filling with thoughts of self-doubt, misery, and turmoil. Having other members of the cult around will also give the person less time to think or rationalize.

During this stage, the agents will then introduce the answer to the person's misgivings. They will force their ideals as the solution to their victims' dilemma. If the manipulators are mind controlling a group, and one or a few happens to have enough sense in them left to oppose the ideas being instilled, they will be isolated or further defamed.

Of course, some would choose to willingly leave the group, and the agents won't stop them from doing so. In fact, this will even help support the cause of the manipulators. They will use this act as a way to uplift the spirits of the remaining victims by saying that the person who walked-out is not yet ready to accept the higher spiritual calling they offer. Those who stayed have evolved or have chosen the more intelligent path.

When the victim undergoes deep and strong emotions, he won't completely be able to think critically, and this is the state manipulators would aim to bring out. Once the people are experiencing misery, they will later on put them in a state of euphoria, furthering the belief they have changed.

Peer pressure is another method that will be utilized by the agents. Exposure to the manipulators' environment with a group will follow these three simple and unspoken rules:

- You will do whatever you say in front of others
- After doing it, you will think of it
- Since you thought of it, you will be under the impression that you have made the decision yourself

And as explained earlier, when you think you have made the decision yourself, the tighter and more solid the new ideals will latch on to you.

Freezing

The pseudo-personality will begin to form in this stage of the mind control process. However, keep in mind that the methods used under unfreezing, the process, and freezing will oftentimes overlap. It will basically depend on how the victims respond to the mind control methods. Nonetheless, during the freezing stage, the person will undergo a struggle because his old and new identity will clash.

In order to solidify the values and beliefs being instilled by the manipulators, they will use the reward/punishment method. Good behaviors will be rewarded by simple yet highly glorifying privileges, like a one-on-one talk with the leader, permission to call his family, or be granted to visit home.

Punishments, on the other hand, are swift but harsh. Depending on how bad the victim's behavior is, but it will range from losing leadership responsibilities, public insults and not being allowed to speak for a whole week. Physical beatings may also be part of the punishment, but, of course, not all cult groups mentioned in the first chapter will do this.

Keep in mind that despite being physically maltreated by his manipulators, the victim is willingly accepting the punishment. He is under mind control, thus both carrot and stick are accepted as is. It's a sad fact that this works but it does.

Another good way to freeze the pseudo-personality of victims is to have them model it. As discussed earlier, the goal of mind controlling cults is to create a replica of the leader. There is no faster way to do this than to have the members go out and recruit people. Through this, they will have to speak with the leader's voice and words in order to get the message through. Selling the idea will, in fact, require the members to be fully invested in it.

Re-indoctrination can also be useful in freezing the pseudo-personality. This is why some cults will require their members to attend seminars or camps every week, month, or year, depending on the 'qualifications' of the group.

The whole mind controlling process is slow, and it may take days to years for it to take effect. Once it does, however, it will also take the same amount of time to undo it, and it may require professional help to do so. The good thing about this is that it's not permanent. As long as the person is removed completely from the mind control environment, or if there are no follow-ups to the process, then it's possible for the victim to get his original personality back.

People often question why women stay in manipulative relationships and the fact is that people in a situation of mind control depend upon the person controlling their mind and don't see it as an option to leave that person, even though their behavior toward them is unacceptable to others. You may even have been in a situation like this and have bought this book to try to avoid getting into that situation again, keeping control of situations yourself. If this is the case, read on because the information contained in the chapters that follow may assist you. They will also assist those who want to take control.

Chapter 3: Mind Control Techniques

The mind control process described in the previous chapter is direct and commonly used by groups or cults of all sizes. There are tons of conspiracy theories fluttering about on the internet, social media, and the likes about mind controlling in a national level. When thinking about the methods discussed, it may seem impossible to conclude that the government, corporations and the elite are, in fact, manipulating the masses. That is because they do a different approach in doing so.

These players are all about power. They do not control the people to earn money and get more recruits. It's more about keeping everyone inline and in their proper places. In other words, it's about maintaining the stability of the system. Though it may not sound as bad because they are keeping things in order, what makes their methods questionable is the fact that they impair people's critical thinking to achieve this goal. Similar with the process explained in the preceding chapter, everyone is under the impression that they have made the decision themselves, that they are living their lives in their own accord.

Most of the techniques they use to control people are all very familiar. If you are an average citizen, then you will know these, and you may have undergone most of it.

Education

As systematic and organized form of education is the perfect mind controlling method any would-be dictator or tyrant would adopt. As justified by how Hitler managed to instill his ideals and beliefs on German minors during his reign, this technique of mind controlling proves to be the most effective.

At such an early stage of life, kids will be taught how to obey and do whatever was instructed. The plausible reason why governing class would want this because is that it will leave every decision they make out of question. Apart from that, whatever mentality they would want to instill will be programmed and will become a part of the original identity of the children. Therefore, if the educational system tells its students that, for example, greed is good, then these children will grow up believing that they need to pursue money and wealth because it is the right thing to do.

Education can also affect the mindset of someone. If a child is brought up in a poverty stricken area, it's quite possible that he will expect less than a child educated in a middle class school who is educated to strive for success. Even though both types of education may encourage a child to strive, one will see being rich as a success while one will see getting out of the ghetto as a success. These are not parallel at all, so education plays a large role in how children's minds see things during a period of great influence when mind control is at its strongest point in their lives.

Propaganda and Advertising

Large-scale mind controlling when sugarcoated is called Marketing. This discipline in commerce is solely focused on knowing what the masses want and need, and how it can play around these two to convince the people that their "wants" are "needs" as well. The main weapon of marketing is advertising and propaganda. Despite having short and brief messages, the way it is structured and composed is centered on conveying messages powerful enough to move people and make them do what it wants them to do.

If different mediums (e.g. television, newspapers, radio, etc.) deliver the same message disguised in different images, and hidden between different sets of words, it will become powerful enough to shape a person's perspective. Advertising does influence the way that people think, as does the media in magazines and even in TV programs. People are effected by what they perceive to be the norm and are influenced to change who they are according to what the norm is.

Religion, Politics, and Sports

These groups work as a mind control technique because it divides the people, and it gives them a false sense of choice -- a word often interchanged with freedom in the modern world. Cooperation can be considered as the government and the elites' greatest fear because when the people unite, it will be almost impossible to win against them.

With the presence of different teams, sects, or parties, the people will more likely oppose each other, leaving the big guys to continue with what they are doing unchecked. For example, the government is always full of issues that need to be settled. Some of them are so sensitive that should the people probe further on it, an uprising or the like could develop. Luckily, however, sports are there to keep the eyes and ears of the masses astray. When everyone is busy cheering for their own teams, they won't have time to listen and seek out more important matters.

As for the illusion of choice, the best example in here would be how people are free to support either the Republican or Democratic parties. Essentially, the two supposedly opposing sides are still predetermined and pre-established. The people are limited in choosing between only two sets of values and beliefs, and yet their freedom to select from the given options is already considered liberty.

The control the elites get from this is a bit messy because it can somehow cause a lot of debates, and series after series of talks and arguments, but it can still keep people in line and away from their rule over the system.

Food, Water and Air

One of the greatest debates currently happening is that of GMO's. The production of food has become so systematic and commercialized that it had to rely on different chemicals and unnatural processes to make ends meet (supply and demand). Because of this, the food being bought almost anywhere literally contains toxins and poisons that can alter the brain's chemistry. Instead of making everyone highly intelligent, however, scientists have discovered that these can lower a person's IQ. Some of the effects of these can extend to an individual's ability to focus. Lacking in this aspect will lead to the person's unmotivated and highly inactive lifestyle.

As described in the mind control process in the previous chapter, one of the techniques used to manipulate people is to limit their food intake. This concept or technique is basically the same. Since this works in the national level, the government cannot actually limit the supply of food to the people; otherwise, they will produce worse results. What they did, however, was alter the components that has the capacity to produce favorable results.

There are other mind control techniques being used on the national level, but most of them are too far-fetched that it will sound impossible or ridiculous for they all seem like science fiction pulled directly from books and movies.

However if you do take a situation such as the way that people think that belong to a religious sect, the strength that people get is from their belief in what they are being told. In some religions, they are also controlled in that if followers do not adhere to the rules set down by that set religion, they can be excommunicated from the religion and that may mean being cast aside by family and friends and having to start again. That's a huge step for people and many will allow the continuance of mind control because it's easier than the alternative.

The point is that if you are going to use mind control, it needs to have a purpose. It needs to give the person being manipulated a reason to stay within the parameters set and for them to believe that it's a very safe place to be. There has to be a lot of logic to the argument and a very good knowledge of the person being controlled because, without this, mind control that is extended over a period of time isn't possible. In small ways, some marriages enter into this area. A partner may change on the wish of another partner because they believe that the security they gain in exchange is sufficient. However, when and if the marriage comes to an end, they have to re-assess their priorities and are often left with years and years of emotional baggage to deal with.

Mind control includes beliefs that are instilled from youth and these may be erroneous values. I remember being of the impression that I should never show my hair when it was wet. It was thought of as unbecoming and that lasted me right through until I was in my early twenties. I was also told many other things which later proved to be of little importance simply because these were my parents' standards. That's quite dangerous, although it wasn't in my case. It's dangerous in that it can pass prejudice from one generation to another and hate for different religions and races, which of course should be left for an individual to decide. Much of the world suffering that we encounter today is due to this kind of mind control and we see a reminder of it on TV every day of the week.

If you think that mind control techniques have nothing to do with your life, take a look at the products that you buy, the religion that you follow and the education you are getting and somewhere among the mix is a certain amount of mind control, whether you want to admit to that or not. We are controlled very much by the environment in which we live and the influences which are brought to bear within that environment.

Chapter 4: Controlling People With Your Mind

Mind control does not always have to be used to manipulate people to satisfy bad motives or intentions. There are ways on how this can be applied in simple ways without any goal of recruiting members and earning money. As mentioned before, this can be used to help cure addiction and even depression. Furthermore, knowing the basics of manipulation can help anyone:

- ➢ Calm down a brewing fight
- ➢ Help a friend undergoing depression
- ➢ Escape the bad side of the office manager
- ➢ Save a falling marriage

There are more situations where mind control can be applied. As long as people are engaged in it, then you can try and manipulate where you want things to end, but it should be used for the general purpose of improvement rather than to try and show superiority.

Know the Personality of the Person

Basically, the first few steps of this are similar with how cults lure victims in -- know the personality of the person. More precisely, you should opt to know how this individual would react to a certain emotion.

Of course, there are other factors in here that should be taken into consideration as well. Think about your objectives. Why would you want or need to control the mind of this person? What are your intentions? And what are the outcomes that you seek?

You need this information, as different character types will respond differently to different tactics. Is your intended victim lured by financial gain, the potential of reward, mental or perceived reward? When you know the personality, you begin to see the route by which your mind control has a chance to work.

Four Basic Personality Colors

Network marketers often categorize people into four types; those driven by pity (yellow), driven by details (green), driven by familiarity (blue), and the last one, driven by competition (red). When they sell to people, they will first initiate small talk and assess where among these four colors the person best belongs to. When they have an idea where, they will then accord their pitch to where the person would best respond to.

To convince yellow people to buy, marketers would need to apply lines like "for charity", "to help a friend", and the likes. They are people high in empathy; therefore, to be able to convince them to purchase a product even if it's clear they don't need it, it should be for a cause.

As for the second one, green people base their purchasing decisions on the effects of the product. What will they gain from it and how will it benefit them? Generally, they are practical, so knowing the science behind the item may come in useful when selling to this kind of personality.

The third ones are probably the easiest ones to sell to. As long as you connect with blues and become their friends, if they have money, they will surely make the purchase. To further the marketers' convincing power, they can add lines like "this will definitely compliment the color of your eyes" and so on. Others will even add names of endearment to further the friendship or relationship.

As for the last ones, reds are the leader-types, and they exude strength and power. To convince them to make a purchase, marketers will have to compare them with other people. Reds are highly competitive by nature and they never want to be overtaken by anyone, so saying lines like "your next door neighbor actually bought three of this" will definitely trigger the need for them to buy the same amount, or more.

If you work out the character types and are able to target them, just as slick advertising does, you are onto a good thing because you will immediately have a head start over people that have no understanding of character types.

The Power of Emotions

Keep in mind how powerful emotions are. This is the very aspect of humanity that moves people -- the one that causes people to act in a certain way. Therefore, if you can induce a certain emotion to a person, then he or she would act based on that. One good example is how you can use guilt to make someone be more considerate towards you.

For example, you got in a fight with a superior in the office. Of course, this can possibly lead to your loss of a job, but if you know how to manipulate the emotions of your boss, then you may be able to save it.

The logic in this is pretty simple. After your fight, if you continue to act like you are right and that you openly express your resentment towards your superior, then the feeling of anger will continue. And as long as this emotion persists, irrational acts such as firing you may become the result. However, if you show that the problem had bothered you negatively and emotionally, then the feeling of guilt will be triggered. When this happens, your boss will be compelled to treat you more kindly.

The situation above is only an example, and there are more emotions that can come at play when you try mind control. There are five basic emotions that can come in handy when you want to practice manipulation, and they are enumerated and explained below:

Fear

This is best induced when aggression is displayed towards you. No matter how big the other guy is, as long as you position your body in a way that exudes dominance, and then the other party may think otherwise with his actions and immediately back out. If you respond with fear, however, expect to be overwhelmed.

Guilt

When a person is angry with you, he will try to destroy you or at least give you a bad day. However, if you can somehow transform that into guilt, then you can expect a semi-special treatment from him or her. This works very well in your favor because the negative emotion of anger often means that those displaying it will have regrets and subsequently will feel guilt. People who are guilty will go out of their way to please you because of that guilt.

Ego

Latching on to ego is good in certain situations. For example, if you find your marriage is starting to fall apart, then openly telling your spouse that people think that. The natural reaction of your partner would be to work hard to prove other people wrong. This can work as well with people who you know are doing things that they would not like to be criticized as ego plays a huge part in their lives.

Addiction

Many would mistake this for something connected to drugs, but it's actually not. There are ways on how to get a person addicted to you; so basically, this is more on mind controlling the person you like to get him or her to fall for you. Addiction means that they cannot live without you in their lives and you can achieve this. Many people do this for the wrong reasons. Look at how people become totally emotionally dependent upon a partner and you will be looking at an example of this kind of addiction.

Anger

There are times when anger can become useful. Like when a person's right is being abused, for example. People can sometimes allow this to happen to them, but if you think it's beyond justice, then you would want to induce anger on that person so that he would be compelled to fight back.

Most of the time, body language will play more significance in controlling other people's minds than the words that you say. So if you plan on taking the practice a bit too seriously, then it is recommended that you read on the subject.

Whether mind controlling is something bad or good, it cannot be denied that everyone uses this is one way or another. Even in its simplest form, the motive to change someone's emotional state is there. However, when used to completely change the identity of a person -- to mold his values and beliefs to something new -- then it becomes something else.

What's important here is that you are given an idea on how people accomplish mind control. Once you are placed in the situation, you will immediately feel the presence of manipulation methods. Whether you would want to join the group, or preserve your identity and personality, the decision will now rest in your hands.

Mind control doesn't have to be negative, but it is always manipulative because you are using your knowledge of the person to get what you want. In my case, after working for three or four hours, I knew that simply picking up an empty cup would mean that my partner would instantly get up and make a pot of coffee. Now, that's a pretty neat trick that hurt no one but which used triggers that gave my partner signals. These are a little like hints but more subtle. It works every time. Why? Because I have a partner who is sensitive to my needs. It wouldn't work on a total stranger because it would not act as a trigger and if you want someone to do something, you need that trigger to be there that puts him or her into action.

Chapter 5: How To Be Deceptive?

Deception can be best defined as the art of concealing your true intentions and showing what you want others to believe. It is the mental act wherein a person actively portrays something untrue while hiding the real thing behind lies and half-truths. This chapter is dedicated to walking you through the subtle art of deception, its various forms and the know-how regarding how to master it to your advantage.

The first requirement of a successful deception is hiding something that is true or genuine. This 'something' could be a hard truth or a fact that could result into you suffering a loss. You can perform the first essential of 'hiding' by various ways. It could be achieved by either remaining completely silent or by deviating the other party's mind towards something else. You can also 'hide' something by covering it up with stories, lies, change of topics and more important facts. However, if you are going to be astute at the art of deception, you really should steer clear of lying because this isn't a great trait to have associated with your name. There are better ways of doing things.

How to Conceal?

You conceal what you fear. Naturally, whatever it is that you are about to conceal has the potential to cause you some sort of loss or suffering. It is because of this nature of the thing that you are hiding that you are choosing to conceal it.

Concealment can be achieved by many ways. To start with, it can be done by completely avoiding the topic in conversation. Let us suppose you were fooling around in your house and accidentally broke an expensive piece of antique vase. In order to hide this mishap from your spouse, you can always take matters into your own hands and create circumstances that will protect you from your spouse's wrath. Rearrange the household arrangement in such a manner that the entire picture is changed in a matter of a few hours. You do not want to face the music when your spouse returns, so you shift some sofas, dust the curtains and completely make your living room a different place. When your spouse arrives, he/she will be so surprised at this sweet gesture of yours that a missing or misplaced vase won't matter to them.

The second requirement of an effective deception is showing what is not true, not entirely so at least. Here comes the most interesting part about deception.

Do not Lie; Tell Half-Truths

In order to really achieve a successful deception, it is not sufficient to have hidden something that you do not wish to be revealed. The next step truly seals the deal as it involves taking that last final step towards deceiving people.

Remember a very important thing about deception. It is not synonymous to lying. Lying is dishonest in nature, while deceiving is done for a greater purpose.

Someone who understands the thin line of distinction between truths and half-truths can appreciate the difference between lying and deceiving. Let us consider an illustration to grasp the concept better.

You are out at a dinner party thrown by your boss. The gathering is there to celebrate your promotion. In the mood for some fun, you decide to exceed your drinking capacity and have more wine than you should have. Your boss offers you to stay back at his place for the night as it gets too late by the time the party is offer. Although there occurred nothing sexual between you two, by the next morning when you return home to your spouse, there are bound to arise awkward moments. This is the kind of situation where you might use a trick or two from the armory named deception.

Remember, deception is not always to gain some unfair advantage over others or to have fun at the expense of others' misery. At times, it becomes absolutely necessary for your survival. Deception is not a new concept. Kings and war heroes have been known to employ the technique of deception to turn the course of our history pages.

The point in this scenario is to clear your name and to give your spouse reassurance, so it's not really negative at all. You could spill the truth if your partner is open to hearing it, but if your partner is definitely not going to swallow the truth, bending it a little to make the peace isn't a bad idea.

The Deception Tool-Box

Let us learn how to use deception in our daily lives, and more importantly how to adapt and change ourselves so as to be able to learn and employ the art of deception to get out of sticky circumstances. It's always handy to know how to do this, though in general, sticking with the truth is always going to be the best option. Sometimes, you are faced with situations where deception actually saves the day.

Develop a dynamic personality

The first thing that people notice when you walk into a room is your personality. Your personality is your resume of sorts. It dictates the next few minutes of your presence and the treatment you are going to receive during it.

A personality is helpful in helping one practice the art of deceiving because a good personality is instrumental in setting up a good first impression. A well established first impression can do wonders if you are looking forward to sway the room in your favor.

Wear simple clothes, walk straight, put a smile on your face, trim your facial hair, iron your suits, do not fumble while talking and assume a straight posture while sitting. Your personality basically builds the base on which your deception skills are going to build an empire! If you don't look like the kind of person who is shady or deceptive, people will not expect deception. A lot is based on what people see and what they perceive from what they see, so looks is everything.

Appeal to Everyone

It is not humanely possible to please everyone. However, it is very much likely to learn how to take no extreme sides in a conversation or a controversy. Your aim is to appeal to everyone in the room. You cannot even think about picking a particular side and start debating with the other. Always balance your views and offer suggestions while talking about an issue at hand. However, if you have already picked a side, stick to it and do not under any circumstance, deviate from it. Make sure you do not end up arguing too much for your side. Try to calm down fights whenever they erupt in a discourse.

Some people have a natural flare for appeal. They are the people who don't make ripples, but help smooth them out. They are people are not rude and who know how to approach people of all ages and get approval. Kids love them. Grandparents approve of them and the average Joe wishes that they could emulate them.

Humor

No one likes an opinion that's insulting AND coming straight. Add a bit of spice to your views by talking in innuendos, and well-timed jokes. If you want everyone to not get offended by your views, you can try covering it all up with things that take up the limelight of the moment. Make jokes and funny insults accompany your statements. People love it when something rude and offensive is also funny at the same time. Instead of getting offended, they end up with their funny bone getting tickled. This is a great way to make sure that you assert yourself and appeal to everyone at the same time.

Chapter 6: Influence- How To Become A Master At It?

All of us want our views and opinions to be not just accepted but also appreciated. However, often to our dismay we discover that it is not always that people around us take as seriously as we wished they did. Do you find yourself being sidetracked and ignored in conversations and life in general? Does something that comes out of your mouth hold more value when reproduced by others in the same way as yours? If you replied in positive to the above two questions, it seems you could use a little help in life.

Welcome to the next chapter that revolves around teaching you some of the best tricks in the book regarding how to build influence brick by brick. Like mentioned above, it is not an easy process. You need to bring some changes in your personality and behavior so as to qualify for seeking influence. Let us start by defining what influence really is and what values it holds in your life.

Influence is the ability to convince others regarding the veracity and truthfulness of your views. Even better, influence is being able to persuading others to let you have your way in a manner that affects even them. Influence has transformed itself from a negative attribute to a tool for survival. Poems and stories might portray the word as something undesirable but in the real world, influence is as necessary to your survival as water.

If you do not have a say in the society in which you live, you are considered a person everyone would rather stay away from. Your workplace demands that you have enough influence to make people listen to you. When you hold influence, you do not need to exercise it. People will work according to your need. The very fact that you hold influence is influential enough. Your romantic prospects increase ten-fold when you come across as someone having influence. Your boss starts noticing leadership qualities in you all because you are someone who has a say in important matters.

If you don't have an influence, start working on it. It gives you clout and when people have clout, others listen to them and are persuaded by them, more so than being persuaded by someone they consider to be a "loser." Would you listen to someone you didn't respect? Would you listen to someone that everyone else dismisses? Chances are that you would not, and that's where influence comes into its own.

What are the benefits of influence?

- ➤ It gets your job done faster and smarter. There are many things that get automatically done just because you are important and possess sufficient influence. When you say, "jump", people ask "how high?" and that means you have sufficient clout to influence others. That matters if you want to use deception. People have to have a reason to believe in you.

- ➤ It saves you time and energy doing work that could have been done in better ways. Imagine the time you would be saving by smiling or frowning and discovering you have pressed the right switch to have your work done. Facial expressions from someone with influence can actually get things moving.

- ➤ It elevates your image in front of those who matter to you. A man with influence is a respected man, they say. Believe it. If you have influence, you can use deception any time that you want to get what you want but use it wisely. Being found out as a liar will not add to your credibility and influence can be lost if you make a mess of it.

➤ Influence wins you favor. Anyone with enough influence is someone people would like to befriend and cozy up to. Such a person usually receives a lot of favors from those who would like to benefit from his influence. You see this every day in business. There are people that turn heads and that have a lot of hangers on wanting to be working with that person of influence. If you are influential, thus it is easier to use deception as a tool to get more from others than they may be willing to give without that deception.

The most common social scenario is a group. Within such a group the most possible activity going on is a conversation. Our lives are filled with such group conversations that happen at almost all places we come across. It could be our office or our local bar. Group conversations are places and times where one could assert oneself and one's views. However, it is often difficult to stand one's ground, leave alone have a say in the group. Let me teach you how to interact in a group so as to sway the situation in your favor.

How to Have your Say in Group Conversations

It is almost an accurate observation that those who start a conversation are also the ones participants listen to the least. Conversations often involving more than two people have a particular pattern to follow. The one starting it usually puts forth the most basic and general matter at hand. The ones talking immediately after them follow the main matter up with added information or opinions. It's those that speak afterwards are expected to bring something revolutionary or different to the conversation. The art of group conversation dictates that you must wait for your turn or keep avoiding speaking unless it's very much mandatory to do so. When such time arrives, you must choose your words carefully so as to not end up offending anyone from the group. Be clever, be witty, but be relevant to what is being said. If you float off topic, then you may not get the audience on your side. The whole point is that you want to influence the conversation, so make your words count.

Remember, you are there to influence others to accept your views. There is a particular manner in which you must carry your conversation. Here are a few tips to so-

➢ Start off by thanking those who spoke before you. It is a simple sign of gratitude that lays the foundation of your first impression. By thanking them, you are suggesting that their values were well received and appreciated by you, which is a good sign and shows sportsmanship.

➢ Do not start attacking others' views despite how atrocious or stupid they were. Put them in a position of reverence and ask them why they said what they said. Do not point out the loopholes in their statements. Try to create circumstances that follow their rules and end up in a massive blunder. Do not conclude your point; let others pause and wonder. The point is to let the opponent make him or her lose influence, not to lose influence by being rude and being a public smart ass. It won't gain any brownie points if you are rude or try to humiliate someone by publically making a spectacle of them.

➢ Having politely destroyed your opponents' cause and words, you are now equipped to lay down your own views. Remember, by now your opponents are seething with revenge and are eager to attack you the first sign of blunder you show them. Be ready for it. Be sure of what you are saying and don't make the same faux pas that they did.

➢ To tackle the above hypothetical situation, start off by mentioning you are not sure about your own ideas. Include a line saying how you are the biggest critic of you. Do not even think about talking about the credibility of your own statements and beliefs. This creates a doubt in the minds of those whom you attacked regarding your true stand. Make sure you tell them that at times your opinions can touch the limits of vagueness and you occasionally get annoyed at how far-fetched they become. They won't be able to bring themselves to bring down a man who has just expressed utter annoyance at his own views. That's a classic trick used by con men, politicians and people who want influence.

➢ The last stage of a group conversation where you are looking forward to making everyone concur with your views is talking. Talking is not the act of doling out words at random. It is the art of knowing what to speak and when. It also includes knowing what NOT to speak. Keep in mind the following points while talking in a group.

➢ Politeness doesn't hurt anybody. A little bit of politeness might just sway others in your favor. If you start off rude, it might upset a lot of people including your opponents, which is the last thing you would want. Sometimes you can control a conversation because of your politeness as no one can show objection to it.

➢ Be concise. A recent study found out that sentences that are five words long have more impact than any other numbered sentence.

➢

Try the following exercise-

A. Power is the best form of knowledge.
B. Power is knowledge in short.

Upon a casual glance, you would notice that the lesser the words in a sentence, the more impact it carries. The number of words in a sentence works either in the sentence's favor or against it. It has been successfully proved that when people use fewer amounts of words in their sentences, they have more mental impact than those who use more.

Everyone loves it when information is summed up in the shortest way possible. Concise and abridged forms of information are not just less hassle to bother with, but also a form of genius and talent. If you are able to express more with the use of very few words, you are adept at conveying what you want in the minimum of resources and effort. This trait in a person shows them in a good light, one that often leads others to believe that you are one to listen to. Such a person is bound to inspire influence.

As has been mentioned before, influence is not synonymous to instilling fear. Here is a scenario to help you understand the difference between influencing and scaring the bejesus out of someone-

James is the boss of your workplace. You are his right hand who gets most of the jobs done. Though officially he handles the department, you are the one doing all the dirty work. People listen to you more than they listen to James. In a company audit, a particular file was found to be containing some sensitive information. The game of finding out the company rat started with James leading the hunt. The rat was found when the person who leaked the information freaked out and tried to shred the evidence and was discovered doing it by his friend, another co-employee. This co-employee came straight to you to report about the rat.

Now normally, in an official set up, everyone reports to the boss but you, being the one with more influence and hence, pseudo-power were preferred over someone who is moody and bossy. The friend who discovered the rat could have easily gone to the boss but he had this nagging suspicion that he'd be safer coming to you with this information.

The difference between having influence and having fear-instilling capacity is that in the former you do not have to be in a position of power or authority however in the latter you have a say only because you have power. You need to understand that being an influential person does not mean that you need to be someone feared and respected. You could be a normal guy with exceptional appealing traits. You should be approachable and friendly. Smiling helps the cause but humor simply doubles it. Learn to laugh with people, not at them. To be a man of influence, you need to be a man of people. Let people trust you to save the day when they have committed their share of blunders.

Another thing that helps gain friends and influence people is never being afraid to admit that you made a mistake. Laughing at yourself is a great way to gain respect because people who are able to do this are also able to be more understanding when others make mistakes.

Leadership is often considered equivalent to possessing influence, and rightly so. When you lead from the front, people start respecting and adoring you. You come across as someone who can not only lead but also when time and situations so demand of you, back down and make the tough decisions. Become a leader and influence is bound to come. However, it is not necessary that every leader is influential enough. Remember, it is leadership and not being a boss. A boss directs people to do the work while a leader works with his people.

In a nutshell, the trait of having influence is not only helpful but also essential to one's survival. In today's world of lies and deceit, it is vital that you have some cards up your sleeve. Influence gets you friends and wins you favor. Being influential is seen synonymous with being a leader. When you have influence on your side, you are highly likely to triumph and rule. It is not a bad thing to have your way. It may be unfair to others but what else is life if not unfair?

Be the person that influences others. Be the go-to person and you can use mind control to make scenarios unfold in the way that you want them to. People will trust you. If you have to use a little bit of deception from time to time, it will be overlooked or not even suspected because it doesn't go with the image of you that people see.

Chapter 7: Tool-Kit For Persuasion

Welcome to that chapter of this book that is bound to help you win at life. Not every one of us is adept at making others see our point of view. At times the need for it becomes so important that we find ourselves clutching at straws trying to find the right way to make our point. This chapter has been specifically written to equip you to realize your true persuasive potential. It's based on business models and also upon models in personal relationships as these have been proven to be very effective when it comes to persuasion levels.

Seem Confident

It does not matter whether you believe in what you are saying or not. It also does not matter whether you are genuinely sure about your point of view's credibility. If you want to persuade others to accept your opinion, the first step is to make a good first impression. The first stage in the direction of this stage is if not being, then at least, appearing confident. If you look and sound like someone who has studied all the aspects and done all his research, people are bound to at least listen to you, if not believe you. Selfoconfidence solves half the problem. The rest can be achieved by following the next mentioned tricks.

Beware, this doesn't mean being a smart ass. People have little respect for those who appear superior and whose attitude is condescending. Make your information enlightening rather than given from a stance of superiority because arrogant people are less likely to get the results that they want. It's worthwhile observing people to recognize the difference and if you do this in a public place and see how people interact with each other, you may notice that the smart ass may think he's on top of his game, but what he is achieving is loss of friends, loss of people's confidence and loss of respect. Do not cross the line between being confident and being a complete jerk by knowing everything. There is a world of difference.

Do your Research

It is absolutely foolish to jump into a persuasive mode without doing your homework on basic and concrete facts. Know what things are true, established and well accepted. Find the weak spot in the facts so found. Without having first gained a thorough understanding of your subject matter it is an unwise choice to walk into a conversation. By displaying that you have read about the issue or you are familiar with it through personal experience, you gain trust of your audience and assure them that you know what you are talking about. I can give you an example here. When visiting an area that I wanted to move to, and without even consultation of my partner, I decided that the only way of achieving that was to show knowledge, to have answers to questions and to make those answers fit with the lifestyle that my partner saw as ideal. A year beforehand, there is no way on earth that he would have considered moving from one end of the country to the other, but because I was able to put a positive slant on it and use my personal experience to persuade my partner, we moved within 6 months and it was me that initiated that idea.

Appeal to Emotions

The golden rule about persuasion is if you can't convince them based on what's true; convince them based on how they feel. It is a universal law of emotions that they are bound to be present behind every action done by human. Emotions are as important as arguments when it comes to persuasive values. If you are faced with the task of convincing someone to give up their life, you can easily do it on sentiments alone. Such is the power of emotions that they can shake up empires and dethrone trade markets.

While doing your research, look for possible opportunities where the audience lost something very dear to them. People have their own weak spots and sometimes such weak spots are common among all. Find this spot and hit it hard. Exploit their emotional ties to something they all hold dear and your words will be applauded and accepted.

Advertisements on television do this all of the time. They look at society norms and they target a certain kind of person. This person wants to be happy or to overcome a problem in life and instead of making a product to overcome that problem, what they do is divert the person into buying something that the person perceives will help them out of that problem and most of the time it's simply a diversion. Think of the emotions of someone who has just been told they have high cholesterol. A message on a TV advert says that they can lower this by buying a certain brand of margarine. They buy into the ideal because they believe it will put something right, but they don't realize that had they simply stopped using butter, the cholesterol level may have corrected itself anyway. Perhaps you can't call this deceptive because there was an element of truth to the advert, but they didn't actually say why you did away with the cholesterol. People go along with what they want to believe sometimes and you can use that in your favor when you are trying to deceive them or mislead them to your own gain.

Use Rhetoric

Rhetoric is that literary tool that doesn't answer a question; it asks another question that nearly answers the first. Let me help you with an example-

Person A- "Gryffindor is the best house at Hogwarts."

Rhetoric reply- "the rest must be quite redundant houses, I suppose?"

When you answer a question with a question, you not only shake the question-asker's credibility but also firmly assert your point. Rhetoric is a great way to win arguments and convince those listening. It also helps you to gain status especially if used when someone you are trying to influence is listening and learning from your methods.

Keep Sarcasm to the Minimum

Sarcasm is an awesome vocabulary trait to possess but at time it can put people off. You cannot expect to win over people by sarcasm alone. You must have true facts and reasonable arguments in your favor too. When you resort to regular use of sarcasm, it may make you appear shady and less confident about your real argument. It also shows a lack of potential to win arguments based on knowledge. Sarcasm is a kind of humor that doesn't fit with a lot of circumstances and if used incorrectly will only gain you a reputation as someone who is unable to take something seriously and that's not a good way for people to see you. You influence no one and are on the bottom of the pile when it comes to being able to persuade someone that something is true, when you know that it is not. You won't be seen as credible and it won't work.

Sound Reasonable

Your point need not be a reasonable one. But your arguments should always sound credible. When you want to persuade people, you must keep in mind that they should feel connected to what you are trying to say. To find this connection, you must start off by adding a bowl full of reason and logic. Make them see fascinating opportunities if they go with your suggestion. But do all this only by sounding reasonable. You cannot persuade people to go beyond their personal boundaries if it's unsafe or risky to do so. A few years back there were companies that were selling holiday dreams to people but making them sound very affordable even to those on limited income. The way that the holidays were packaged was in such a way that people saw the possibility of their dreams coming true. Did they in fact come true? Perhaps they did, but the intention of the company was simply to sell a dream. In some cases, people found that the reality was very far distant from the dream that was envisioned. Package something in such a way that it meets people's needs and they will go for it. Credit card companies do this all of the time. It's not actual deception but by goodness be sure that you look beyond the advertising because in the small print, you may find the cost of having all that money at your disposal is much more than you planned on spending in the first place.

I gave these examples because they show how sounding reasonable gives responses that are positive. There were adverts recently that targeted people who were overweight offering them a pill that made them slim without having to change their diet. Do they work? Of course not, but people having been swallowed into the dream feel foolish and it's hardly likely that they will ask for a refund because it makes them feel even more foolish so companies such as this make a fortune out of deception. You see photographs of before and after the treatment but look carefully at the angle from which they were taken as many were taken in a photographic studio in the same photographic session. However, the angle at which they were taken and the stance of the model made a difference. It looks reasonable. The photos look reasonable and thus people are able to persuade others on the basis of reasonable evidence, even if that evidence is totally fabricated.

Watch Reactions

When you are amidst a persuasion session, you cannot go on and on about the point you are trying to make. Learn to take mild pauses so as to allow yourself the chance and time to judge people's reactions to what you are saying. Look for signs of distrust or dissent. Some people might be disagreeing with you but because of how busy you are proving your point, you might not notice them at all. This further helps the build their case against you.

It is important that you go ahead based on how your audience has been reacting so far. If disagreement pops its heads up in forms of moans, murmurs and sighs, make sure you change the direction of your words. Tweak your tone and try to steer away from what you think is causing such disturbances. A great political way of dealing with bad reactions is to confront them. This gives people the impression you are not trying to hide things and may be used to persuading those who were in disagreement that they might have judged you too quickly. Don't flog a dead horse. If the reactioon to a suggestion you make is obviously not going to get what you want, adjust your approach because you haven't presented the idea in a way that persuades and persuasion is what deception is all about.

Subtlety is the Key

Even when you are in the right and you are aware that no argument in the room could challenge your statements, do not go full hulk on the audience or the opponents. It is the sign of a good speaker that he is subtle and gentle in his words and manner in which they are presented. Work on the art of subtlety. Subtlety is used in all kinds of situations and it takes common sense argument in a much more logical sequence so that instead of shouting from the rooftops "I am right and you are wrong" and creating hostility, you are saying "it would seem that ..." and back this up with facts, statistics or anything else that you need to push your message home.

Cross out the Alternatives

In a particular issue, there is numerous numbers of solutions. However, you are supposed to be the advocate of just one. While you are at it, it will be for your benefit to point out the loopholes in all others. Tell your audience as to why you think the solution that you are offering has no other good alternatives. Walk them through existing alternatives and show them why they should not be preferred over what you are arguing in favor of. Strike away other solutions with artsy presentation and sarcasm if you must, but make them realize that your way is the best option they have.

Alternatives are always going to leave doubt. In a recent campaign to sell detergent or cleaning products, one of the main manufacturers did this, crossing out products that were on the market and telling the audience why their product was better. This is a known way to persuade someone in favor of your argument.

Suggest!

Persuasion is not about telling them to not do it; it's about showing them what then? You cannot walk in, disprove everything they believed in so far and walk out expecting people to take you seriously. Persuasion hasn't even started by the time you are done with attacking formerly held beliefs. The real act of persuasion lies in offering them what you think is the real way out to the problem at hand. After having convinced them that what they had been doing so far was a result of bad choices, it's time for you to lead them towards good ones. Always end your persuasion with what you think is best for the subject(s) of your persuasion. Until you put in the effort to make some advice of your own, no one will be truly convinced with what you just said.

Persuasion is one vital aspect of mind control. It is the subtle art of making people accept your point of view, despite how flawed they may be. Not everyone knows how to persuade a crowd. However, the art can be learned by following some simple tips. Learn not to go headstrong into a conversation.

Sit back assess the situation. Know your enemies and your friends. Discover the weak points, both in people and in points. Appeal to as much number of people as possible. Be gentle yet firm in your views. Assert with confidence what you believe in. Attack politely and back down when it's required. Apologize for your mistakes and accept your flaws if they are proved. If you want to be a good persuader, become a good learner first.

Listening

One of the best tools that you have with being persuasive is the ability to listen to people. This is potentially the most important piece of equipment you have in your deception toolbox. If you don't take time to listen to people and to observe them, you have no actual reason to believe that you know the ideology of the person you are trying to persuade. People types, characters and values are all important to someone who wants to persuade. You must have seen how gullible politicians think that voters are when you see the politicians holding babies in their arms.

They may not really be interested in listening to what parents want to say but they want to give off the impression that they understand mothers and the problems that families have. In fact, this ploy is so outdated that it doesn't really work that well any more for winning votes. A better way forward for them would have been to listen to what people are saying and to use that for ammunition of persuasion. If people think they have been heard, they are much more likely to be able to be manipulated. They trust people who listen to them and make them believe that their point of view actually counts for something.

Observation

This tool is also very useful for those who want to deceive others into doing what they need done. Observation shows you the character types; it shows you who people listen to and what they are saying about different aspects of their lives. Observation helps you to single out the right person to do what you need to be done the first time, rather than making a fool of yourself by picking incorrectly. There are obvious types of people with obvious types of belief systems and you can be much more persuasive if you have the intuition to be able to recognize character types. Don't assume you can do this through common sense. Sometimes you get it badly wrong. Learn from observation and your persuasive skills will improve tremendously because you will begin to approach the right person first time instead of making mistakes.

The above skills will help you to be able to manipulate situations successfully. No, we don't like telling lies and using deception, but sometimes it is a necessary evil to get things done. If you use all of the tools that we have given you in this chapter, then the chances are that you will not only be able to achieve, but you will set an example to others as to how achievement improves your situation.

As a last tool toward using persuasion, it is always worth joining a debate society because these teach people how to win arguments and also help you to hone your argument skills in order to persuade people of the right of the side that you are arguing on. I remember at University, the debating society was one of the most useful of tools that I had at my disposal and knowing how to bring something up and change people's views about something really helped me to become influential and to take my thoughts and put them into words that people of all types were able to trust as being good information.

In the political arena, you see all kinds of arguments and you know from the look of a candidate whether he is speaking from written pages or whether he's speaking from something that he actually believes in. Even those of a different political persuasion may be persuaded to change their vote if they see this kind of sincerity and belief. Even though you know that you have to use deception to get where you want to be, the greater good should dictate your purpose so that the results benefit everyone.

When you are able to produce results like that, then you really can use deception and persuasion to get what you want out of life or out of a work situation without making people feel that they have been used. It's a case of persuasion plus respect for your opinions being stronger than someone's unwillingness to do something. Suggestion can also help to move mountains as it's putting ideas into someone else's head and letting them put those ideas into action, though the power of the suggestions that you make.

Chapter 8: Tips To Playing Mind Games

This is my favorite part of the book. Here we will learn how one can change or modify one's personality in order to be in the right position to play mind games on people. One thing that needs to be kept in mind is that not all mind games are harmful. Some of them are also aimed at giving you advantage of various kinds.

Prefer Half-Truths over Whole Truths

You do not have to say the complete truth. You can always choose to conceal something important and mention that's not so. By doing so, you won't be lying but simply not saying the full truth. You can always claim that you didn't lie if caught some time later. However, if the situation calls for it, do not be hesitant to speak half the truth and conceal the rest. This works particularly well when someone asks you a direct question to which you do not want to give the full answer but do need to come up with some kind of answer. Half-truths are not exactly lies and you can always claim that you didn't think that element of the truth was important at the time if you are caught out.

Appear Introvert

Most winners are introverts. It is believed that introverts are mostly intellectual, reserved and possess a high degree of mental capacity. You can use this wrongly held belief to your ample advantage by simply appearing introvert!

If you are walking into a new social group of friends, make sure you appear an introvert from the very beginning. Extroverts are not really welcome at groups that already boast of established member roles and interpersonal relationships. Extroverts are threats! Do not take the garb of an extrovert. Choose to at least seem like an introvert at first. It is very important to stay reserved for future use also. Introverts are easily trusted as they mostly keep to themselves.

Talk less

The more you talk, the more people judge. By deciding to limit the words that come out of your mouth, you will be essentially giving others few opportunities to assess you. In order for you to be a master of deception, you must make sure that you are not easily readable by a lot of people. The best to ensure that is to start off by restricting your talking.

Hit when the Iron is Hot

It is not sufficient to put a tape on your mouth and impede your talking frequency. You are not supposed to stop speaking! Learn to pick up the right moments when you talking might have a deciding say in the course of the conversation being held. Say, you are out with your group of friends and someone brings up the topic of apartheid. Having paid less attention in social studies class, you have negligible idea about the issue and yet you are compelled to speak. Resist the temptation for now. Wait for the right and appropriate topics to come up and then choose to display your knowledge or vocabulary.

Be Selective; Not Choosy

Set apart standards for you. Be very selective in who your friends are and with whom you share your secrets with. However, do not overdo this selection act otherwise people will see you as someone who's just trying to appear classy and choosy. By showing that you are really particular about your company, you sort of build trust and interest in people surrounding you. You come across as interesting despite you not being really so. This leads to what you speak turning into something precious. This, in other words is called influence. Influence is built, not gained overnight. This building of influence takes time and patience. However, you can tweak your personality in such a way that influence isn't difficult to gain access to.

Gain Trust

In order to play with people's trust, you need to gain some first. It is a tricky thing to gain trust in the first place. You can start off by doing people favors and offering them things and services for free. However, trust is gained best when you spend time with people. If you want to take advantage of people, you have to spend a lot of time with them and make them believe that you are one such person in whom they can blindly put their trust.

However, one golden rule of mind games dictates that breaking someone's trust must be avoided till the last extent possible. Even if you have done something deceitful try to hide it for as long as possible. You can always save yourself some trouble by taking measures to make sure the trust you have so patiently gained is not revealed to have been broken. Pro tip- Shift it on someone else's head; if possible, someone you would like to see in trouble.

Mind games are played not for fun but for gaining personal advantages. It is totally okay to look for personal gains in this world of competitions and lies. Do not loathe yourself for seeking personalized goals and aims. The purpose of playing mind games can vary from evading a potentially harmful situation to gaining edge over competition. Everything is fair in love and war and life is a bit of both. Try to not offend people while you are at it though. As they say, keep your friends close but your enemies closer. Do not underestimate others' capacity to spot deceit. Remember, everyone's on red-alert all the time. Play your games but look out for possible traps. You may be falling into a booby trap and not know it yet.

Chapter 9: What Is Manipulation and What Are Its Benefits?

Manipulation is the art of carefully engineering circumstances to work in your favor. It is the practice adopted by those who have all odds stacked against them. But any average man is known to have practiced manipulation in some form or the other. Consciously or otherwise, we manipulate things and people throughout the day. We may not realize that we are doing it, but it's there. If you sat at the end of the day and try to recall all those situations in which you swayed people to work for you or under you, you would be surprised at the their frequency.

Manipulation is therefore, a good tool to possess. Its benefits are various, some of which have been listed below-

1. Manipulators get their way around things. They are never the ones who have to compromise with people or situations. They know how to get their work done in tight circumstances.
2. Those who manipulate are destined to succeed at life. These are people whose dictionaries do not contain the word 'failure'. Nothing is over until the curtain declares that they are the winners.
3. Manipulators know how to avoid tricky situations. Not only do they almost successfully prevent them, but also tackle them if prevention is not possible.
4. Manipulators make the best out of the worst. If you are aware of the tricks of the trade, you will know how to have your way through the stickiest of mazes.
5. Execution of a plan requires not just knowledge and talent but also a bit of manipulation. It could be any plan- your office work, household or neighborhood. Any plan requires a master Manipulator who can take care of things related to deceit and stealth.
6. Manipulators have power. They are not the ones hogging the limelight but those working behind the curtains. They will come across as normal human beings with smiles plastered over their faces. But behind those pretty faces

are hidden some sinful and really brilliant plans to extract the best out of the worst.
7. Manipulation is a great source of self-confidence. You might not think very high of yourself but once you have managed to have your say in matters then you will automatically feel self-confidence surging inside of you.
8. Manipulators are prepared for the worst sort of situations. They know how to wiggle out of the trickiest corner and hence they are always on their toes awaiting danger or threat.
9. Manipulation builds your success, except brick by brick. Having manipulative say is not sufficient; building a network based on manipulation is.
10. Manipulation digs up your hidden potential to win at life. Not only does it increase your chances to succeed but it also makes you do things you never imagined you would do.

Moral fix

Do not get into a dilemma regarding using of manipulation as a tool to have your way. It may so happen that you being a righteous person may find the use of manipulation a bit inconsistent with your beliefs and practices. You need to disassociate yourself from such morally uptight principles. You may notice that the world has moved on and no one's to be trusted.

The world runs on lies and secrets. Learn to gather as much as you can on the other person's personal lives and use it to your advantage without feeling guilty about it. If something when used works in your favor, but harms someone else, you need to first measure the amount of damage caused. If such damage is material in nature, then you might reconsider your step. However, if such damage is negligible and really does not affect the damaged party, you should totally go ahead with it.

Morality and practicality rarely go together. The more morally uptight you become, the less practical you turn into. It is for your benefit that you become as objective as possible. Of course being objective does not mean elimination of emotions and reason from your mental scope. It simply means giving preference to logic over everything else.
Use the best available to you. If there is an opportunity for something to be used, do it.

Do not let go of chances for second chances are a mummer's dream. Manipulation is a man's that side that prompts him to use situations to his advantage and pleasure. If you lack manipulation, you may succeed but you will have a tough time keeping succeeding.

Chapter 10: How To Manipulate

Welcome to the next chapter. Here we will deal with the various ways in which you can manipulate people around you. Of course you cannot expect to learn the art overnight but a little bit of observation and a bit of patience will do the work.

Observe

The first step to learning anything is to observe. When you observe you pick up things you had missed out on before. The following are some examples of what to observe-
Observe how people react when subjected to certain conditions or emotions. It is by decoding people's behavioral pattern that you can come across the key to their control-room.

Notice the emotions people display in specific circumstances. Pain, Love, Hatred, and Anger have different impacts on different people and everyone has their own way to respond to emotion. Tap into these emotions and keep a record of them.

Observation is half the job done as it makes you familiar with how people think and analyze their behavior according to the stimuli received and the expected response to it.

Let the other party speak

Remember, the first rule of manipulation is that you speak as less as possible. When you speak, you let people have access to your thoughts, views and mental state. When you are so exposed that your actions start indicating what you are thinking, you no longer enjoy the trust of those who considered you a consistent and stable minded person.
It is only the one who speaks less and listens more who gets accepted as a reliable person to divulge matters in. Be that person and you will gain the perfect chances to be in a position to manipulate.

The Less you Reveal; the more they Wonder

The worst thing you could do to harm your opportunities to be the master manipulator is show all your cards that you have got up your sleeve. Once you have opened your hands, you are an uninteresting person. Always keep the other parties guessing your next move. Add in some unpredictability and you are good to go.

The best Manipulators are the Best Speakers

When you speak, you basically let the other party know of what you are thinking. When your thinking is shown to others, they are assured of your reliability and skills. You may not be genuinely skilled or resourceful but your speaking skills will more than compensate for it.

Be Subtle

Subtlety is the art of the classy. When you say something straight it might come across as rude or worse, misunderstood. Go for a touch of subtlety instead. Subtlety is the practice of saying something in a way that does not present itself upfront.

Subtlety is often misconstrued as sarcasm. The difference between the two is the while the former is non-offensive the latter is necessarily meant to be offensive. The purpose of subtlety is to not leave any chances of offense, while the idea behind the usage of sarcasm is to mandatorily make sure that offense is conveyed clearly.

Appeal to Emotions

One of the best features of manipulation is its usage in terms of sentiments. Emotions drive almost every human action possible under the sun. Be it conquest or civil war; emotions are always involved in everything.

Now that you are familiar with the fact that emotions are behind almost everything, you can use this to manipulate emotions to your advantage. Do your homework about the emotional weakness of your audience. Your research must cover all the previous experiences of those listening to you. Grab hold of these aspects of your audience in order to have your say in how they react. Watch their reactions as they sit through your speech. Change the course of your speech according to the varying degree of audience response.

Be Suggestive and not instructive

It is a simple rule of psychology that when you directly tell people to do something or refrain from something they are least likely to adhere to your instructions. However, if you suggest it instead of telling, people are likely to listen to and follow it.

Instead of saying something like "you should do this work", you could replace it with "Maybe you could try doing this work? It is really up to you."

Cleverly bring out the negatives

If you want to prevent someone from choosing a particular option, be clever about talking about its negative points. Include the positive points as well but show them that the cons outweigh the pros by a good margin.

Conclusion

Manipulation, deception, half-truths and mind control are closely related to each other and form parts of your daily lives, whether you know it or not. You may not know it yet you may be practicing it right now. There is a difference between lying and the mentioned aspects of mental features. Lying is direct, straight and done without much planning.

On the other hand, deception and manipulation is a developed mental practice that once incorporated into your mental faculties will offer you the best possible ways to have your way in life. Do not ashamed of or reluctant to use the methods provided in this book in order to shape up your life to a better form.

The end justifies the means. It does not matter how you reached your destination or achieved your target as long as you reach there or acquire it. The benefits of having reached your end outweigh the criticisms that you might receive for having used means that are generally considered immoral, unconventional and contrary to popularly held beliefs.

In today's world of astute materialism and objectivity, you must mold your behavior to suit the changing needs. Guilt will only push you backward. There should be no scope for you to feel guilty about using the methods so prescribed in this book. Remember, the purpose is to reach the end, no matter how you do it.

Thank you for choosing this book. I hope you enjoyed the journey!

You May Enjoy My Other Books

Author Page

http://hyperurl.co/Jeffdawson

PSYCHOPATH: Manipulation, Con Men And Relationship Fraud

smarturl.it/psychoa

Boundaries: Line Between Right And Wrong

hyperurl.co/boundaries

NARCISSISM: Self Centered Narcissistic Personality Exposed

hyperurl.co/narc

Personality Disorders: Histronic and Borderline Personality Disorders Unmasked

hyperurl.co/borderline

BODY LANGUAGE: How To Spot A Liar And Communicate Clearly

hyperurl.co/bodylang

Tantric Sex and What Women Want - Box Set Collection: Couples Communication and Pleasure Guide

hyperurl.co/sexwomenwant

Boundaries In Marriage: Line Between Right And Wrong

hyperurl.co/marriage

Boundaries: Crossing The Line: Workplace Success and Office Sex

hyperurl.co/crossline

Personality Disorders: Psychopath or Narcissistic Lover?

hyperurl.co/psy

Boundaries: Parents and Teenagers: Sex, Privacy and Responsibility

hyperurl.co/boundariesteens

Printed in Great Britain
by Amazon.co.uk, Ltd.,
Marston Gate.